NE

TI^{THE}GERS

NEVER MIND THE TIGERS

The Ultimate HULL CITY QUIZ BOOK

PHIL ASCOUGH

The History Press

This book is for those people who give their lives to football. The relatives left at home while loved ones traipse to both home and away games following their team; husbands, wives and children who can't book holidays until the fixtures come out. Over time they have come to terms with the fact that Saturdays are not great for weddings but now find themselves having to also think twice about Sunday to Friday because football is now even more unpredictable, and not in a good way.

Specifically it's for my family. For the parents, brother and sister I grew up with, and for my wife Jayne, son Matthew, and daughter Amber, whose sporadic interest in the beautiful game stops some way short of true passion — especially if Dr Who is on.

First published 2013

The History Press
The Mill, Brimscombe Port
Stroud, Gloucestershire, GL5 2QG
www.thehistorypress.co.uk

© Phil Ascough, 2013

The right of Phil Ascough to be identified as the Author
of this work has been asserted in accordance with
the Copyright, Designs and Patents Act 1988.

British Library Cataloguing in Publication Data.
A catalogue record for this book is available from the British Library.

ISBN 978 0 7524 9764 8

Typesetting and origination by The History Press
Printed in Great Britain

Contents

	Foreword by Burnsy ...	7
	... And Swanny	8
	Assists	9
	Introduction	11
Round 1	Cup Glory	15
Round 2	Fer Ark	18
Round 3	The KC Stadium	20
Round 4	Our Guests	23
Round 5	We'll Never Play There Again!	26
Round 6	Easy Balls	29
Round 7	Fish	32
Round 8	Battered	36
Round 9	Gaffers	39
Round 10	Striking Tigers	42
Round 11	Between The Sticks	46
Round 12	Long Punts	50
Round 13	We Are Premier League	53
Round 14	No Easy Games	55

Round 15	Yorkshire's Number One?	58
Round 16	The World Stage	61
Round 17	Tiger Nations	64
Round 18	England Expects	67
Round 19	Home Internationals	70
Round 20	Tap-Ins	73
Round 21	Club Connections	76
Round 22	Loan Stars	78
Round 23	The Nearly Men	82
Round 24	Tiger Teeth	86
Round 25	Tiger Tantrums	90
Round 26	Crunching Tackles	94
Round 27	Tigers on TV	97
Round 28	Celebrity Tigers	100
Round 29	Christmas Crackers	103
Round 30	And Finally …	105
	The Answers	109

Foreword by Burnsy ...

Oh, I only wish Phil had pulled his finger out and got this book published ages ago. He would have saved me some sleepless nights. I've compiled the odd quiz and have woken up in a cold sweat, trying to think of questions and, more importantly, answers, and this would have saved all the effort. Therefore, I appreciate the time and research that's gone into exploring the nether regions (just past Anorakville) of the Tiger Nation!

This book will also be accompanying me into the commentary box for City games, with a two-fold purpose: one, dipping into it for a little trivia to entertain our audience in any dull moments, although the football is rather less dull in Hull these days. And two, clipping Swanny round the ear with it when he steps out of line.

Mentioning Swanny – he doesn't do quizzes!

... And Swanny

Hi, this is Swanny – ahem … former record signing at three Football League clubs, read my book for detail. I don't do quizzes, but if I did, this is the book I'd steal. Sorry – buy!

David Burns has been commentating live on Hull City matches for BBC Radio Humberside for 20 years. As summaries became an essential part of live coverage, Burnsy was joined 10 years ago by Peter Swan, a veteran of nearly 400 Football League appearances. Swanny also writes for the Hull Daily Mail *and is the author of* Swanny: Confessions of a Lower League Legend, *published by John Blake, 2008.*

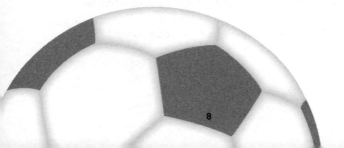

Assists

Having worked in the media for more than thirty years, writing and contributing to a good few football books along the way, I can't say I was too perturbed at being asked to compile a Hull City quiz book.

But as I only started watching the Tigers on a regular basis after moving to the city in 1980, I knew it would be reckless to embark on such a project without the aid of a safety net. I doubt whether Trevor Bugg has ever been called that before, but he'll know what I mean.

So the themes and the questions are all mine, as are any errors and subsequent apologies. What Trevor did was help to sharpen a few facts here and there, clarify the odd reference point and provide an invaluable sounding board for some of the more unusual content ideas, exactly as he has for previous projects by me and other authors.

And what of those other authors? Well, there's Mike Peterson, whose Hull City books are as fascinating as they are illuminating. I've been thumbing through *Tiger Tales: A Who's Who of Hull City AFC 1904–2000* and *A Century of City: The Centenary*

History of Hull City AFC 1904–2004 (both Yore Publications), and I look forward to reading them properly and enjoying in full the remarkable stories that lie behind the comprehensive statistics.

And there's Chris Elton, whose *Hull City: A Complete Record, 1904–1989* (Breedon Books Sport) is another gem. I particularly like the section on friendlies – a flashback to the days of occasionally exotic overseas tours and clashes with top clubs, who usually fielded a few big-name players.

But a lot of football history is gradually finding its way onto the web, which brings us back to Trevor. As one of the key members of the team at www.11v11.com, Trevor works tirelessly to make sure their database on Hull City and other clubs is as up-to-date as it can be.

It is a never-ending task but a vital one, because without it we risk losing sight of the fact that there is football life beyond the Premier League and that from April 1963 until September 1998, Hull City were unbeaten in ten games against Halifax Town.

Many thanks to all of the above and, of course, to Burnsy and Swanny.

Introduction

So, you're huddled round the table in the pub, mood dictated by whether it's pre- or post-match, anticipating excellence, fearful of failure, celebrating victory or drowning sorrows. Someone throws in a question, and off you go …

Who was in goal when …? Who scored when …? Who got sent off when …? Who got locked up when …?

And the last thing you need is someone from the club telling you to leave that question out because it's too controversial, or the know-all at the next table pointing out that it wouldn't be proper to mention George Boyd playing for Scotland while on Hull City's books without also crediting Mike Gilhooley in 1922.

So this Hull City quiz book is neither official nor definitive. And it's entirely possible that by the time you read it one or two of the questions and answers might have been overtaken by events, because football is like that – it doesn't stand still, even if some of the players do.

It is intended to be a celebration of Hull City, our club, players, fans and opponents, and of football generally. Hopefully it's also a bit of fun.

The format is straightforward enough: thirty rounds of eleven questions each, every round with a theme of sorts and the whole thing building a picture of Hull City's highs and lows.

Some questions are so straightforward you'll be able to rattle them off in the time it takes to review Mark Hateley's managerial career. At the other end of the scale, one or two are harder than Billy Whitehurst. But please don't tell him I said that.

There is no attempt to provide any sort of historical balance, because it would be daft to overlook the fact that very few readers will have a chance of nailing questions about the Raich Carter era, never mind pre-Second or even First World War.

But nor does this book get carried away with the Tigers' Premier League years. Certainly, compiling the book was far less arduous a task and the outcome far more interesting as a result of City's two years in the top flight, but even newcomers will be aware that the Premier League experience was all the sweeter because of some of the perils of the past.

We saw mock funerals before they were fashionable, repeated receiverships and closure threats on the way to being locked out – twice – of the tumbledown ground that was supposed to be one of football's cathedrals.

Such recollections are not intended to make light of the catastrophes endured by other clubs and their subsequent efforts to rebuild, but there is no doubt that the feeling of ecstasy which results from success is sharpened by memories of the occasions when Hull City might have slipped out of the Football League or even out of existence.

So treat this book as you do the Tigers: enjoy the journey. And if you feel like taking a detour while negotiating one round or another then be my guest. Hull City players with fruity connections rather than fish? Why not? Another eleven football grounds that we'll never visit again? At least! A Tigers A to Z? You can do that one yourselves.

Phil Ascough, 2013

Cup Glory

Because we can be quite good at irony. And it's Round 1 because, in the finest traditions of Hull City, we've decided to get the FA Cup out of the way and concentrate on other stuff. We'll maybe look at the other cups later. If we can be bothered.

1   Which was the last team from a higher division to be knocked out of the FA Cup by Hull City?

2   What forced the abandonment of City's FA Cup first round tie at Runcorn in November 1993?

3   City made it as far the third round of the League Cup
    in 1997, but in the same season lost in the FA Cup first
    round to which non-League side?

4   Which non-League side did City beat in a second replay in
    the FA Cup second round in December 1980?

5   Which striker scored against Cardiff City, Bradford City
    and then Liverpool as the Tigers memorably fell at the
    fifth round stage in 1989?

6   At which ground did City draw 0–0 with Whitby Town
    in the FA Cup in 1996 before winning the replay 8–4 at
    home?

7   City reached the FA Cup semi-final for the only time in
    their history in 1930, but were beaten in a replay by which
    team?

8   Which national event coincided with City's FA Cup quarter-final replay against Chelsea at Boothferry Park in March 1966?

9   In 1905 City won their first FA Cup tie as a Football League side 8–1 against which 'brassed-off' village team from South Yorkshire?

10 Who were the last team to beat City on their way to winning the FA Cup?

11 In the 1960/61 season, City's FA Cup run extended to seven games, including five matches – one of which was abandoned – against which side?

Round

2

Fer Ark

When it opened, Boothferry Park really was ahead of its time. Long before the Tigers moved on, it had fallen into crumbling decline and certain parts of it really didn't smell too good at all. When a stray ball – or perhaps a Justin Whittle clearance – flew towards the roof of the West Stand, regulars would place their match programmes on top of their heads to protect themselves from the shower of falling rust.

1   Why do some people refer to Boothferry Park as Fer Ark?

2   What was the name of the first supermarket which opened on the site of the old North Stand?

3   Which Hull-born former secretary of the Football League in 1964 officially opened the gymnasium which was built behind the South Stand?

4 Who were the opposition and what was the score in the first match at Boothferry Park in 1946?

5 For which sport was the site of Boothferry Park used before the construction of a football stadium?

6 Six were available but only four were used when City beat Barnsley 7–0 in October 1964. Four what?

7 Who were the first visitors to lose a league match at Boothferry Park and also became the last to win there?

8 Which opposition player featured in the last match at Boothferry Park and the first at the KC Stadium?

9 Who were the last visitors to Boothferry Park in the FA Cup?

10 Which routine was presented for the first time by match day announcer Martyn Hainstock ahead of a make-or-break match against Cardiff City on Friday, 9 October 1998?

11 Who were the visitors in January 1951 when the first trains ran to Boothferry Park Halt?

The KC Stadium

Harold Needler promised City a state-of-the-art stadium and, at the time, Boothferry Park wasn't far off. But Adam Pearson, along with a lot of help from Hull City Council, finally delivered with the KC Stadium, and in doing so triggered a transformation in the club's fortunes. It is remarkable to think that from opening in 1946 until relegation to the Fourth Division in 1981, Boothferry Park had only hosted matches in Divisions Two and Three, including Three North. The KC saw City begin 2003 in the Fourth Division and end 2008 in the Premier League.

1   Against which team did City record their highest attendance at the KC Stadium?

2   Who scored City's first hat-trick at the KC Stadium?

3   Who, in October 2004, became the first City player to
    be sent off at the KC Stadium?

4   Against which team did Nick Barmby score the quickest
    goal at the KC Stadium after just seven seconds of play in
    November 2004?

5   In January 2010, who were the scheduled opponents
    for the only City match at the KC Stadium to have been
    postponed?

6   Which team has inflicted the most defeats on City at the
    KC Stadium?

7   Which referee, later a Premier League regular, officiated
    for City's first defeat at the KC Stadium, a 1–0 loss to
    Lincoln City in February 2003?

8 City and Sunderland competed for a trophy named after which former manager in a friendly match on opening night at the KC Stadium?

9 Which defender scored City's 100th goal at the KC Stadium, the first in a 2–0 win over Colchester United in February 2005?

10 Why was City chairman Paul Duffen left red-faced as he conducted a ceremony to mark promotion to the Premier League, ahead of the first match in August 2008?

11 Which pop superstar and football fan played the first major gig at the KC Stadium in July 2003?

Round

4

Our Guests

Hull City owner, Assem Allam, added a new event to the KC Stadium's repertoire with the British Squash Open, but City's home grounds already had a long tradition of hosting other events, from international football and rugby league matches to the performances of global pop stars. Yet not all of the activities were entirely successful.

I   Which sport made an appearance at Boothferry Park in the 1950s but never returned, mainly because of the damage it caused to the pitch?

2   Which future Scotland manager played for his country's youth side against England at Boothferry Park in 1958?

3 Which rising star of international management led a Football League XI which beat a League of Ireland side 5–0 at Boothferry Park in October 1965?

4 Why was Boothferry Park the venue for a top-flight match for the one and only time in 1971, when Leeds United played Tottenham Hotspur?

5 In 1972, who were Northern Ireland's opponents for a European Championship qualifier which was played at Boothferry Park because of security concerns in Belfast?

6 At which sport did Great Britain play France at Boothferry Park in August 1980, as part of the Humber Bridge Festival?

7 Which team staged exhibitions of basketball skills at Boothferry Park in 1956 and again in 1983?

8   In the final of which competition did Hull FC beat Hull
    Kingston Rovers at Boothferry Park in October 1984?

9   Which invitational all-star cricket team played Twenty20
    cricket against Yorkshire at the KC Stadium?

10 Which future Premier League star was the captain of
    the Netherlands Under-21 team, which lost 3–2 against
    England Under-21s, at the KC Stadium in February 2004?

11 Which rock band played at Hull City Hall in 1970 and the
    KC Stadium in 2007?

We'll Never Play There Again!

Many famous old football grounds have gone the way of
Boothferry Park, particularly in recent years. We'll miss some
more than others, and we'll have fond memories mixed in
with the tales of freezing, rain-soaked misery, because many
away ends had a certain earthy charm – even Donny, which
unfortunately doesn't make this selection.

1   What was the venue for City's only away match against
    the MK Dons?

2   Which City striker scored in each of the team's last two
    visits to Plough Lane, Wimbledon – a 4–1 win in April
    1984, and a 3–1 defeat two years later?

3 Which midfielder scored one of his fifty-four league goals for City in a 2–1 win over Brighton and Hove Albion in August 1965, which was the club's only victory at the Goldstone Ground?

4 Which TV pundit scored twice as City lost 3–0 in a Littlewoods Cup tie, which was City's last visit to Highbury?

5 Peter Skipper scored the only goal of the game as the Tigers sealed promotion from Division Three at this West Midlands ground which was demolished in 1990. What was the name of the stadium?

6 Which team did City defeat 3–1 in the last night match to be played at their old ground, as the Tigers marched towards promotion to the Premier League in 2008?

7   Which team suffered their first defeat at their new
    stadium when the Tigers claimed a 2–0 win in September
    2005?

8   Who scored the vital goal for City to earn their last win
    at Ninian Park, Cardiff, in April 2007?

9   City's last visit to this Yorkshire football ground brought
    a rare goal for Rob Dewhurst in a 2–0 win. Name the
    ground.

10 City played only four matches at this ground, which was a
    temporary home for their hosts for ten years from 1986.
    The last visit was a 3–1 defeat in the relegation year of
    1996. What was the ground called?

11 City lost at the home of these fierce and controversial
    promotion rivals in November 2000, and made only one
    more visit there – a 1–1 draw in the 2004/05 promotion
    season. What was the name of the ground and the team?

Round

6

Easy Balls

The first of our random selections, tinkering with the line-up, and with no real pattern or strategy – how many times have we seen that on the pitch? More than enough but not for a while, thankfully. Anyway, here are eleven general questions that shouldn't be too taxing to answer.

1   Prior to taking over at City, which non-League club did Don Robinson lead to victory in the FA Trophy in 1976 and 1977?

2   Which burly striker did City sign from Mexborough Town in 1980?

3   Which former rugby league player was installed as Chairman of Hull City by new owner David Lloyd in 1997?

4   In which competition did City lose to Manchester United in the first ever penalty shoot-out in British football in 1970?

5   Which defender-turned-striker – who 'doesn't do quizzes' – arrived at City as the club's record signing and made his debut in a 3–0 win over Plymouth Argyle in March 1989?

6   In 1981, which team did City meet in a friendly as part of the Humber Bridge Festival?

7   What was the name of the second 'Reggae Boy' who joined City, along with Theodore Whitmore, in 1999?

8 Against which team did City record their record-low home attendance of the post-war era, for a match in the Auto Windscreens Shield, in December 1996?

9 Who was City's first million-pound signing, and from which club did he join the Tigers?

10 Which player scored City's first hat-trick for nearly four years, in a 5–1 win at Scunthorpe United in February 2011?

11 As assistant manager to Warren Joyce, John McGovern helped to keep City in the Football League. With which club did he win the European Cup twice as a player?

Round

7

Fish

Proof of just how difficult it is to shed a stereotype comes with the fish thing. The port of Hull hasn't had any fish for a while, and what's more, the Tigers haven't even had many people with fishy names or connections. Other teams can call on a Haddock or Perch, a Ling or a Pollock – we can't even find a John West, so some of these are … well … fishy.

1   A tap-in for starters. There was a time when some fans considered filleting and battering to be a soft option for this guardian of the club.

2   The miniature striker and play-offs veteran who scored the last of his eight Tigers goals from the spot, against one of his former clubs. But there was no champagne or misspelt caviar.

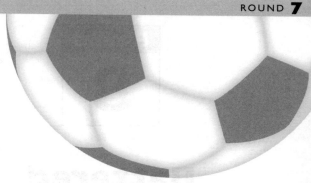

9 Hull City's most famous fisherman, who reportedly netted £45,000 a week.

10 The solid and occasionally spectacular keeper who featured in some of City's biggest matches during four seasons with the club. Couldn't keep out Leyton Orient in the play-offs, but managed a clean sheet in the first game at the KC Stadium.

11 Spent a couple of spells with the Shrimpers and was also a Gill before preparing City to challenge the big fish; he subsequently slipped back into the shallow end.

Round
8

Battered

Not in the sense of Eric McManus, the unfortunate Bradford City goalkeeper who fell to the ground with a dull thud and a rattle of rearranged bones after a collision with Billy Whitehurst. This one is about those mis-matches which left one side chasing glory and the other chasing shadows.

1   Who were the victims when City recorded their record League win of 11–1 on 14 January 1939?

2   Which future City manager was on the scoresheet when the Tigers were hammered 6–0 at Aston Villa in August 1974?

3   Duane Darby scored six as City beat Whitby Town 8–4 in the FA Cup in November 1996. Which players scored the other two?

4 City's record-breaking side of the 1965/66 season netted 109 League goals. How many players reached double figures? Can you name them?

5 Who scored on his debut as City beat Kidderminster Harriers 6–1 in September 2003?

6 Which former Tigers midfielder finished the game in goal for the visitors in December 2004, when City beat Tranmere Rovers 6–1?

7 Who scored a hat-trick for City in their 7–1 victory over Crewe Alexandra in October 1994?

8 Who lined up for Colchester United in a 5–1 win over City in November 2006, but joined the Tigers the following season to help City's push to the Premier League?

9 Which goalkeeper started for City in the 1953 team that beat Oldham Athletic 8–0 and was still there in 1958, when the Tigers went one better to beat the Latics 9–0?

10 Which midfielder scored his only goal for City in the 5–0 win over Southampton in March 2008?

11 Which City defender scored an own goal in the 6–1 FA Cup defeat at the hands of Chelsea in December 1999?

Round
9

Gaffers

If continuity is the key, then it is easy to see where Hull City have been going wrong. After Manchester United appointed a relatively fresh-faced Alex Ferguson as manager in November 1986, the Tigers had 18 changes at the top during his near-27-year reign. Each of them, at some time or other, had something to cheer about. Iain Dowie's sole victory is covered elsewhere.

1 Who is the only man to have managed Hull City twice since the Second World War?

2 Which former City manager's playing career included spells with AC Milan, Monaco and Ross County?

3 Which manager was hailed as the most expensive scout in City's history, lasting only 17 games in the Boothferry Park hot seat, but managed to sign Stuart Green, Ian Ashbee and Stuart Elliott in that time?

4   Name the three managers used by City during the
    1977/78 season.

5   How many times did Billy Russell act as caretaker
    manager between 2000 and 2002?

6   Which City boss reached the rank of Major in the Army
    and kept the title throughout his career in football
    management?

7   Which City boss was sacked after a 4–1 home defeat
    by Swindon Town and then rejected an offer of
    reinstatement?

8 Who was City's longest serving post-war manager?

9 Which manager took Wales into the last eight of the European Championships – and City into Division Four?

10 Former City bosses Terry Dolan and Eddie Gray also managed which other Football League team?

11 Which City manager's party piece was an impression of Norman Wisdom?

Striking Tigers

City have actually had a few decent strikers don the black and amber over the years. Lately the problem has been finding them. Years ago it was more an issue of hanging onto them. There was even a time when things became so bad that Terry Dolan sent the keeper on to make a nuisance of himself up front …

1   From which Scottish Premier League club did City sign legendary goal scorer Stuart Elliott?

2   Dean Windass left Boothferry Park for Aberdeen in December 1995, but with which club did he return to the Football League in August 1998?

3   This striker scored 25 League goals for the Tigers in the
    1990/91 season, but the rest of the team only contributed
    32 between them and City were relegated. What was his
    name?

4   Age and injury limited the contribution of this giant
    centre forward but he became a legend anyway, scoring
    five goals in 22 games in the 2000/01 play-off season.

5   Which player announced his arrival at the team with a
    goal on his debut against Exeter City in November 1964,
    and would eventually become the Tigers' talisman during
    eleven years with the club?

6   Which team paid City £92,000 for Chris Chilton in 1971?

7   Name the Aussie international who was one of three
     players to score on their debut, as the Tigers thumped
     Darlington 4–1 on opening day in 2003.

8   Who was the only City player since the Second World
     War to score 30 League goals in a season as the Tigers
     won promotion from Division Three in the 1958/59
     season?

9   Not what you'd call prolific, but 11 of this striker's 19
     goals for City came during the Great Escape season of
     1998/99, and were vital in helping the club stay in the
     Football League. Who was the striker?

10 This player scored all three goals for the Tigers in a 4–3 defeat at Workington in 1956 three years after he'd bagged an historic hat-trick in a famous Cup final, but what was his name?

11 Alan Fettis was yet another hero in goal for the Tigers, but was pressed into emergency service as a striker – how many goals did he score in the 1994/95 season?

Round

11

Between
The Sticks

In recent seasons, City have almost had enough loan goal-keepers to comprise an entire starting XI. But for our focus on the men between the sticks, it is only fair to concentrate on those players whose Tigers' stripes had a degree of permanence, even if their spell in goal was only temporary.

1   This player, a central defender by trade, filled in when the first-choice keeper picked up an injury on the way to a Full Members Cup tie at Southampton in 1986. In the starkest of contrasts, the Saints had Peter Shilton in their goal. Can you name the City keeper?

2   Name a City legend from this one-word clue: Oranges.

3   It is easy to forget that Boaz Myhill took some stick when
    he was City's number one, but he remains a firm favourite
    of the Tigers' fans. From which club did City sign him?

4   This keeper made 456 appearances for City, including
    403 in the League. The Second World War interrupted
    his thirty-four-year career with the Tigers – what was his
    name?

5   Steve Wilson was never the first choice for the number
    one shirt, yet spent ten years with City while supposedly
    better keepers came and went. But where did Willo go
    when he finally left?

6   Apparently slightly taller than Willo but looked the size of Dean Keates, this import from Portugal played only one match for the Tigers in a 2–1 Carling Cup defeat at Blackpool in 2005. Can you name the player?

7   Name the highly rated keeper who made 240 League appearances for City and later earned a chance at Manchester United. He is also known for having misjudged a long kick to concede a goal to Bristol City keeper Ray Cashley.

8   A Welshman, signed by City's former Wales manager and only denied more appearances for his national side by the class and consistency of Neville Southall.

9   Plucked from a non-League team by Warren Joyce in 1998
    and sold a year later to Derby County for £460,000 – a
    welcome and much needed cash injection – name the
    keeper who became a City saviour in more ways than one.

10 Roy Carroll was effectively sold twice by the Tigers, for
    the initial fee of £350,000 followed by a knock-down
    payment to eliminate a potentially lucrative sell-on clause.
    Who were the purchasers?

11 The last goalkeeper to captain City made 91 League
    appearances for the Tigers after signing in 1988. Who
    was he?

Round

12

Long Punts

Here's another collection of bits and pieces that don't quite fit in anywhere else, although comparisons with Junior Lewis may be a little harsh. Some might say he played a key part in getting the Tigers through some tough games in the battle for promotion in 2004. As you might expect, there is less certainty about the outcome of these Long Punts than the earlier Easy Balls. If you don't know the answer, just have a guess.

1   In the penalty shoot-out defeat to Manchester United in 1970, which Old Trafford legend missed his spot-kick?

2   Which midfielder, who spent his entire professional career with City, served as the captain from 1981 until 1988?

3 Who were City's opponents on Saturday, 3 May 1980 –
the day that Hull FC and Hull Kingston Rovers met in the
Rugby League Challenge Cup final at Wembley?

4 Which Hull City manager made his only appearance as an
England player in a 2–2 draw against Wales in 1975?

5 Which unwanted record was set by City centre-half
Arthur Childs in 1930?

6 What model of car was presented by Hull City to Terry
Neill when he joined the club as player-manager in 1970?

7 What was significant about City's 2–1 win over Leeds
United at Boothferry Park on 22 December 1985?

8   What forced the postponement of the Third Division match between City and Notts County in October 1961?

9   What was the price of the match-day programme when Boothferry Park hosted the First Division match between Leeds United and Tottenham Hotspur in August 1971?

10   Prior to introducing bylines for their Hull City reporters, what was the pen name used by the *Hull Daily Mail* for reports of the club's matches?

11   Why did City keeper Jacob Iceton remain on the field when all the other players had left during a reserve match at Doncaster in 1926?

Round

13

We Are Premier League

During the early months of 2008, the laziest cliché in football was the one about Hull being the biggest city in Europe never to have had a top-flight football team. So we buried it, and for the last few months of that year set about shaking up the Premier League. This is a round of celebration.

1   Who scored City's first goal in the Premier League?

2   How many goalkeepers did City use in Premier League matches during their two seasons in the top league? Can you name them?

3   Which player made the most Premier League appearances for City?

4   In which month and year did Phil Brown win the Premier League 'Manager of the Month' award?

5   Against which team did City achieve their only Premier League double?

6   Who scored an own goal on the last day of the 2008/09 season to preserve City's Premier League status, at the same time condemning Newcastle United to defeat at Aston Villa and relegation to the Championship?

7   Which City player was ever-present during City's first Premier League season?

8   Who scored City's winner in the memorable victory at Arsenal in September 2008?

9   Against which team did Dean Windass score his only Premier League goal for City?

10 Who scored his only goal for the Tigers in a 2–1 win over Manchester City in February 2010?

11 Who scored City's last goal in the Premier League before relegation in 2010?

No Easy Games

And then the wheels fell off. True, City were never really in danger of doing a Derby, and there were no defeats to challenge the Premier League record books. But there were constant reminders of how tough the competition can be, when even a team that has never finished higher than tenth can hammer you in your own backyard.

I   Sam Ricketts deflected a corner from which opposition player into his own goal to set Wigan Athletic on the way to a 5–0 victory?

2   Which City player scored the first goal of the 2009/10
     Premier League season in a lunchtime kick-off at Chelsea?

3   Three Premier League strikers feasted on City's defensive
     shortcomings by helping themselves to hat-tricks during
     the second Premier League season. Name any of them.

4   Who scored for City against Middlesbrough in December
     2008, and for Boro against City the following April?

5   Who scored City's equaliser before they crashed to a 6–1
     defeat at Anfield in September 2009?

6   Which City player scored four own goals in Premier
     League games between December 2008 and November
     2009?

7 Only one opposition player scored more Premier League goals against City than the answer to number 6. Who was he?

8 Which player made his last City appearance in the 5–1 defeat at Manchester City on Boxing Day 2008?

9 Who was the only City player to be sent off twice during the Tigers' time in the Premier League?

10 Unlucky or what? How many Premier League matches did Jimmy Bullard start for City?

11 Which player scored his only Premier League goal for City to give them an early lead against Burnley in April 2010, before the Clarets hit back and won 4–1?

Round

15

Yorkshire's Number One?

Except it's not as simple as that. All the mucking round with Humberside has muddied the waters somewhat, and the fact is that our closest rivals geographically are in Lincolnshire. So this round looks at them, as well as some of the Yorkshire clubs who have tried and failed to finish higher than City in recent seasons.

1   Which defender-turned-striker lined up for York City on their last visit to the KC Stadium in February 2004 and subsequently joined the Tigers in 2006?

2   Waggy scored twice when City beat which local rivals 3–2 on the opening day of the 1965/66 promotion season?

3   Which Yorkshire rivals hosted City's FA Cup replays against Blyth Spartans in 1980 and Rochdale in 1981?

4   City haven't played Grimsby Town in a League game since 1987, but in which competition did the sides meet in 1998?

5   One half of the 'Smash and Grab' duo who never quite clicked at City, with which Yorkshire club did Alan Warboys begin and end his football career?

6   Who scored two goals – including a sumptuous volley – as City won 4–2 in December 2004 in a memorable first match at Hillsborough for 14 years?

7   Who were the beneficiaries in the 1984 Division Three promotion race when City, needing to beat Burnley by three goals in the final match, only won 2–0?

8   Which midfielder, who was often criticised for his goal return, netted both home and away as City did the double over Barnsley in the 2007/08 promotion season?

9   Fans of which Yorkshire rivals united with City supporters in an attempt to burst a police bubble?

10   Which Yorkshire neighbours were the visitors for a 1999 relegation battle which attracted City's biggest home crowd for eleven years – recorded as 13,949 but estimated by many to have been much higher?

11   What was controversial about Bradford City's visit to Boothferry Park in May 1996?

Round

16

The World Stage

There is nothing quite like the World Cup. For all the rows about host nations, qualification stitch-ups and boring group games, we'd be lost without the culture, colour and no small amount of class that comes around every four years. City have had a few who have played their part at some time or other, and who largely reflect the ups and downs of the tournament itself.

1   Which player, who later joined the Tigers, scored England's first ever goal in the World Cup finals, scoring the first in a 2–0 win over Chile in 1950?

2   Literally a big name signing for City. Which player went to Germany with the Netherlands for the 2006 World Cup, but played only the last six minutes of their knockout defeat against Portugal?

3 Which City player was ever-present for Ireland at the 2002 World Cup, but was one of three players to fail to score from the spot as they lost out to Spain in a penalty shoot-out.

4 Name the Aussie who competed at the 2010 World Cup while still a City player but who headed home early after the Socceroos were eliminated at the group stage.

5 In his short spell with City, this player became a firm favourite at the club and showed glimpses of the magic that took him to three successive World Cups with Nigeria. Who was that player?

6 Which player scored twice in 1998 as Jamaica beat Japan 2–1 to record their only win at the World Cup?

Round

18

England Expects

In all honesty, England has never really expected much from Hull City and has therefore never been particularly devastated when the club have failed to deliver. The Tigers have had a few connections with the national side, but usually via those who rose to prominence after leaving the Tigers, or those who dropped in on their way down.

1   Making more than 80 appearances for the Tigers after signing in 1949, this player is remembered more as a controversial figure for his antics as manager of a team who were big in the 1970s and for his spell in charge of England. What was his name?

2   Who scored six goals in 11 League games for the Tigers, 10 years after emerging as a star striker at Southampton, where he earned two England Under-21 caps?

3   Pilloried for his time as England coach and for his dodgy
     Dutch accent, Steve McClaren was a classy midfielder
     with City. Where did he go when he left?

4   Brian Marwood began his career with the Tigers but it
     wasn't until 1988, by which time he was with Arsenal,
     that he earned international recognition. Against which
     opposition did he win his solitary England cap?

5   Who was the former England captain who came in to
     steady City's defence as they closed in on promotion
     from Division Four in 1983?

6   The Second World War restricted Raich Carter's
     England career to 13 games, from which he delivered the
     impressive return of seven goals. Against which Home
     Nation did he make his debut in 1934?

7 Which English contemporary of Carter's made 26
   appearances for the national side but fell foul of FIFA
   by signing for Colombian side Santa Fe in 1950? On his
   return he joined the City squad.

8 Which player, who later signed for City, was a non-playing
   member of the England squad in 2008, two years after
   offering his services to Jurgen Klinsmann on the basis of a
   German grandmother?

9 Nick Barmby scored the first goals of Glenn Hoddle's
   and Sven-Goran Eriksson's international reigns – against
   which nations?

10 As caretaker manager of England in 2000, who did City
   manager Peter Taylor appoint as captain for the first
   time?

11 Which striker made his England debut in 1976, two years
   after leaving Boothferry Park?

Home Internationals

Strictly speaking this should only cover those Tigers who played for England, Northern Ireland, Scotland and Wales, but convenience – and the number of players in recent years – dictates that the Republic of Ireland should be included, especially as City really haven't fielded many Scotland internationals as of late.

1   Name the diminutive but combative midfielder who played 31 times for Scotland and joined City's coaching staff in 1977.

2   Boaz Myhill represented England at lower levels before committing to Wales, but in which country was he born?

3   Thierry Henry admitted that he handled the ball to
     score for France while under pressure from which City
     defender during a World Cup qualifier in 2009?

4   Keith Andrews, who later became a Republic of Ireland
     favourite, joined City from Wolverhampton Wanderers
     in 2005, but where did he go next?

5   Sam Ricketts became a firm favourite with the Tigers and
     a regular in the Wales side. Who is his famous uncle?

6   Jon Walters has made his mark in the top flight with
     Stoke City and on the international scene with the
     Republic of Ireland, but with which side did he make his
     Premier League debut before his spell with the Tigers?

7   Name the stylish Wales midfielder who began his career with Wimbledon's 'Crazy Gang' and played a handful of games for City in the 1997/98 season, scoring four goals?

8   Which City player made his Scotland Under-21 debut as a substitute against Sweden in August 2010?

9   Former Tigers boss Terry Neill is tied with which other former occupant of the City hot-seat on 59 caps for Northern Ireland?

10   Name the Republic of Ireland international who was City's top scorer in their second Premier League season.

11   Which Greek Super League side signed former City and Northern Ireland keeper Roy Carroll in 2012?

Tap-Ins

Welcome to our third miscellaneous round; a heady mixture of exotic places, Tigers legends, big names from the world of sport and a former Chairman who, until his arrival at City, was best known for fighting people while wearing swimming trunks and a mask. Nothing in this round is as tough as that man.

1   Which former Scunthorpe United Chairman was voted City's 'Supporter of the Year' after leading the consortium that purchased City from David Lloyd in 1998?

2   What is the name of the trophy contested by City and North Ferriby United in a pre-season friendly every year?

3   Against which Hungarian side did City pull off a shock win in a friendly at Boothferry Park in October 1955?

4   Who left the job of assistant to Hull City manager Terry Neill in 1971 when he was offered the chance to manage the Scottish national side?

5   Under which name did former Tigers Chairman Don Robinson perform as a professional wrestler?

6   Which player was ever-present in League games for City for five seasons from 1983 until 1988?

7   Which Florida side did City beat 3–1 on aggregate in a friendly challenge for the Anglo-American Cup in 1984?

8   Which England cricket international played in the Scunthorpe United team which were beaten 1–0 by City at Boothferry Park in December 1983?

9   Which player was City's top scorer in League games in the 2006/07 season – 12 years after he previously held the top spot?

10   Which City striker scored on his debut against Southend United in August 2002 and went on to be the leading scorer in three out of four seasons?

11   Who succeeded Justin Whittle as the Tigers captain, and held the job for eight seasons?

Club Connections

Perhaps there was a time when it would have been relatively easy and possibly even entertaining to pull together 11 questions on players who dedicated their entire careers to Hull City. But not for a while, so instead have a look at each group of players and name the club other than City for which they played.

1   Peter Swan, David Beresford, Gordon Staniforth.

2   John Hawley, Iain Hesford, Roy Greenwood.

3   Matt Glennon, Michael Bridges, Les Mutrie.

4   Brian Marwood, Jackie Sewell, Richard Hinds.

5   Alan Warboys, Jamie Forrester, Darryl Duffy.

6   Dennis Booth, Bryan Hughes, Alex Dyer.

7   Terry Curran, Pat Heard, Kevin Kilbane.

8   Andy Saville, Sam Collins, Eddie Blackburn.

9   Clayton Donaldson, Dele Adebola, Neil Franklin.

10   David Brightwell, Geovanni, Alf Wood.

11   Linton Brown, David D'Auria, Richie Appleby.

Loan Stars

You don't need to have a particularly good memory to recall the buzz of excitement that would grip City fans every time the club brought in a loan player from a big club, or even a modest club that was in the Premier League. These days the deals tend to be for months at a time, or even a full season. Some work out, some don't, but can you name them?

1   Made more than 200 appearances for Arsenal and 14 for England, struggled with a succession of clubs in the Premier League era but lit up Boothferry Park with his classy performances when he arrived on loan in 1997.

2   Came in from Aston Villa in 1992 and delivered six goals in 13 games. A six-figure move to Stoke City followed, but he couldn't maintain such an impressive ratio and called in at clubs including York City, Darlington and Scunthorpe United on his drop down the divisions.

3   After relegation from the Premier League led to the loss
     of Boaz Myhill these two keepers came in on loan during
     the first season back in the Championship.

4   A player who was tipped as a star of the future when he
     arrived at City in February 2006 and to be fair he has
     shone at West Ham United. But he only completed 90
     minutes in two of his five matches for City.

5   Loaned to City by West Bromwich Albion for the run-in
     at the end of the 2007/08 season. Recalled when it
     became clear the Tigers actually had a chance of catching
     The Baggies at the top of the table.

6   This quick Bermudian striker, who started his English career at Scarborough in 1992, finished it on loan at City 10 years later, and in between made more than 300 League appearances, mainly for Walsall, Stoke City and Macclesfield Town.

7   One of the few players revered by fans of both Merseyside clubs, his career would have taken a different path if City had been able to afford him after a loan spell from Liverpool in 1986.

8   This midfielder demonstrated, while on loan at Cardiff City in 2010, precisely why you should always include a clause to prevent your players lining up against you for the opposition.

9 Signed on loan from Rangers in 1998 and scored three goals in 12 games for the Tigers, but this was the era of David Lloyd and Mark Hateley and there was never really a chance of making the move permanent.

10 A loan deal which did evolve into a permanent move. This big striker scored on his debut at Brentford in February 1999, went back to Lincoln City but returned to City in time to play his part in the Great Escape.

11 Signed on loan from Stoke City in 2009 and took his place in a defence which conceded 10 goals in his first two away games. A bit harsh to blame him for the failings, but a lot of people did.

23

The Nearly Men

Message boards, online forums and good old-fashioned gossip and speculation will always generate any number of spurious links between clubs and players. At unfashionable City, the transfer rumours rarely make the national headlines, but over the years there have been some bizarre tales about moves that were never going to happen, and some that nearly did. Can you name the players who nearly wore the black and amber stripes of the Tigers?

I   A star both north and south of the border, whose career included three spells with Middlesbrough. The *Hull Daily Mail* actually embarked on a car chase, pursuing Hull City officials to try and get pictures of the meeting, but the deal never happened.

2   Another hugely ambitious signing with City apparently
     willing and able to splash out around £12 million to one of
     La Liga's top clubs. But again, the deal never happened.

3   He reportedly agreed a deal in February 2013, went for
     lunch and returned a few weeks later playing for the
     opposition – he ended up on the losing side.

4   A star in the Premier League and with England and
     strongly linked with the Tigers when Newcastle United
     dropped into the Championship in 2009.

5   The story goes that City only signed Billy Bremner in
     1976 because this equally combative midfielder opted for
     a move to the south coast when the time came to leave
     Arsenal.

6   In his day he was a tough midfielder; as a manager he has
    been linked with City on a number of occasions, with
    fans, perhaps harshly, split between those who don't want
    him and those who really don't want him. Oh – and he's
    not Peter Reid.

7   A hero and villain with the England side, this player was
    something of a late developer before making his name
    primarily with Nottingham Forest.

8   A highly respected striker, he managed the remarkable
    achievement of being a fans' favourite at Arsenal and
    Manchester United. Apparently he came very close to
    joining the Tigers in the early 1970s while hanging around
    in The Gunners' reserves.

9   The one who nearly left the Tigers. Chris Chilton was
    believed to be heading for Elland Road, but the deal was
    off after Don Revie signed this other centre forward in
    1967.

10 The arrival of Steve Bruce as manager was always going
    to generate rumours that this former England striker and
    veteran of more than 500 Premier League appearances
    would follow, but he went to play in Australia instead.

11 His goals made the difference in the 2008 promotion
    campaign but he was never Hull City's player, and a lot of
    fans really don't like him for going elsewhere.

Tiger Teeth

For all of the considerable pleasure we take from watching a an artist of football at work, mesmerising the opposition with weaving runs, defence-splitting passes and audacious chips to leave a goalkeeper stranded, we love our tough guys and it is so, so tempting to just come up with 11 questions based around the answer to number 2. Can you name these 'tough' men of City football?

1   He played his last game for City in 1967 but is regarded by those who saw him as one of the hardest and most committed players ever to wear the black and amber.

2   A fearsome striker who had two spells with City in the 1980s and earned a reputation as one of the toughest men in the game. The rumour that he once punched a horse cannot be easily dismissed.

3   A player whose seemingly untamed aggression in the
     heart of City's midfield brought him a couple of red cards
     in the 1999/2000 season. He collected another on his
     return to Boothferry Park as a Torquay United player in
     2001.

4   Never a dirty player, this midfielder picked up only one
     straight red card in two Premier League seasons with the
     Tigers, and that was later rescinded. However, City were
     certainly a tougher proposition with him in the team.

5   A busy midfielder as player-manager and almost a
     grandfatherly figure in later years as assistant manager,
     but whether in the middle of the field or the post-match
     press conference, this City stalwart could be as hard as
     nails.

6   Six red cards in City's colours and it would have
     undoubtedly have been more but for the career-
     threatening injuries which this legendary midfielder
     overcame as he defied seemingly impossible odds again
     and again.

7   An Aussie international who only played 10 matches
     for the Tigers and picked up a goal and a red card in the
     second of those – a 2–1 win over Rushden and Diamonds
     in February 2002.

8   Arrived midway through the 'Great Escape' season; this
     ex-Army man battled his way to the 'Player of the Season'
     award and was the fans' favourite in a team not short of
     heroes.

9   According to Walsall's website this defender is their
    senior physiotherapist. Sadly it was injury which limited
    his capabilities by the time he arrived at City at the end of
    1998, and it's entirely possible he sustained it by running
    through brick walls.

10 Born in East Yorkshire and not the biggest, but he earned
    a reputation as a hard-working midfielder and then a
    battling boxer not to be messed with, even on Twitter!

11 But boxing titles are no match for the Military Medal
    awarded to this full-back for bravery at the Battle of
    the Somme in 1916. He also received the Distinguished
    Conduct Medal and Bar, and in 1919 he signed for Hull
    City, beginning an association which would last fifty years.

Tiger Tantrums

On the pitch, City have, with one or two exceptions, notably against Arsenal, usually been models of good behaviour to the point where it's not easy to recall major controversies. Off the field is rather different, and while certain issues over accommodation of fans are covered elsewhere there have been plenty of other headline-grabbing episodes involving players, supporters and club officials.

I   This player's goals helped to keep City in the Premier League but the relationship between him and the club was always an uneasy one. A bust-up with other players was one factor in his loan deal being terminated, and more serious matters subsequently brought a jail term. Who was the player?

2   Dean Windass was booked in bizarre circumstances at
     Stoke City in November 2008. What did he do to upset
     the officials?

3   Which Arsenal player was cleared by the FA after being
     accused of spitting at the end of the FA Cup quarter-final
     against the Tigers in March 2009?

4   What were the City fans' missiles of choice for a protest
     against David Lloyd at the Worthington Cup tie at Bolton
     Wanderers in September 1998?

5   Which City player staged his own protest against
     disgruntled fans by running to the empty Kempton stand
     to celebrate both his goals in a 3–0 win over Brighton and
     Hove Albion in March 1997?

6   City's home defeat against which local rivals in October
    1996 sparked pitch invasions by angry Tigers fans during
    and after the match?

7   Members of which esteemed organisation reportedly
    witnessed a post-training, warm-down spat between Nick
    Barmby and Jimmy Bullard at the Humber Bridge in March
    2010?

8   Jimmy Bullard became locked in a prolonged legal battle
    with the Tigers after being suspended in 2011, following
    an incident at a pre-season training camp in which
    European country?

9   The sale of which piece of Hull City's heritage, in order to raise desperately-needed funds in 1994, caused uproar among fans when it was revealed in 1996?

10 Who sold Hull City but kept Boothferry Park and locked the club out of the stadium in 2000 and again in 2001?

11 At which Premier League ground did Phil Brown infamously deliver the half-time team talk on the pitch with the Tigers trailing 4–0?

Crunching Tackles

It's time for a final random collection of highlights from Hull City's history; from famous match facts of years ago to obscure observations from around the edges of more recent events. Even the chap who is the answer to number 4 might just struggle with a couple of these.

1   Who were City's opponents for their first floodlit Football League match in April 1956?

2   Julian Johnsson signed for City in 2001. For which nation did he make more than 60 appearances?

3   Which future Hull City managers were sacked by Bradford City after the Tigers knocked The Bantams out of the FA Cup in January 1989?

4 Which statistician and ardent Tigers fan was the author of a regular feature in the Hull City match-day programme entitled 'Quality Balls'?

5 Against which team did Chris Chilton earn his first representative honour as captain of an FA XI in 1968?

6 Against which team and at which venue did City play their first professional football match – a 2–2 draw in a friendly in September 1904?

7 On a tour of which British overseas territory in 1988 did City's opponents include Dandy Town and Pembroke Hamilton Club?

8 Which club did former City manager Colin Appleton serve with distinction as a player, leading them to their first major honour with victory in the League Cup?

9 Which current Scottish Premier League side lined up against City for a fund-raising match, after the loss of fifty-eight men on board three Hull trawlers in 1968?

10 Against which team did City record their only win in nine matches under Iain Dowie's guidance in 2010?

11 When City secured promotion with a goalless draw against Swindon Town at the KC Stadium in 2005, which player missed the penalty that would have sent the Tigers up in style?

Round
27

Tigers on TV

The myth is that the Tigers always fail on TV. True, it took some time for our camera-shy heroes to register in front of a nationwide – or even global – audience. And someone, somewhere, will surely have a live TV league which will have City languishing deep in the bottom half. But some of our biggest wins have been shown on the telly; matches that we'll never forget.

1   Who were City's opponents in their first live televised game, a 3–1 defeat in the Zenith Data Systems Cup in November 1990?

2   An injury to which Bristol City player forced a lengthy delay when City won in front of the cameras to claim a place in the Premier League in May 2008?

3   Who were the opponents for City's first live TV game in the Premier League? Where? And what was the score? WHAT WAS THE SCORE?

4   Against which Premier League side did City lose 3–0 at the Workers' Stadium, Beijing, in a live TV match in the Barclays Asia Trophy in July 2009?

5   Against which Yorkshire rivals did City achieve their first live TV victory, coming from behind to win 2–1 in a Championship clash in September 2006?

6   Which player scored with a deflected shot at the KC Stadium as City lost 1–0 to Aston Villa in January 2006, the Tigers' first FA Cup tie to be shown live on TV?

2   The answer to number 1 was also influential in securing
the support of this world famous actor, who insisted on
meeting Ken Wagstaff when he came to Hull in 2010 to
receive an honorary degree.

3   A graduate of Hull Cricket Club, a reliable bowler on the
county circuit and a highly successful coach.

4   If this TV presenter had turned up in the Boothferry Park
days she'd have spruced it up in no time. In between fixing
the roof, plumbing and electrics, she also finds time for
Tigers-related tweets.

5   Popstar Sinitta told Radio Humberside she became a fan
of the Tigers after being charmed by this former City
striker.

6   A couple of these chart-toppers are City fans and can often be seen mingling with fellow diehards, but the front man is definitely a Sheffield United fan.

7   This Tigers fan found fame with high profile TV roles in such series as *Please Sir!* and *Upstairs Downstairs*, but not as much as he did for narrating *Fireman Sam*.

8   Too easy, but a list of celebrity City fans would not be complete without this playwright who died in 2010 and whose works included *Confessions of a City Supporter*.

9   The man who succeeded Derek Fowlds as Basil Brush's sidekick has always preferred Tigers to Foxes.

10   Born and brought up in California, this guitarist with indie rock band Pavement ended up being a Tigers fan but countless interviewers never seem to have asked him why.

11   When City signed goalkeeper Maurice Swan from Drumcondra in 1963 they secured the support forever of this young, future leader of the Irish government.

Christmas Crackers

As recently as 1967-68 it was not unusual for clubs to play each other twice over Christmas, often on consecutive days and with no regard for the distances involved. It was a combination which produced some bizarre results. On Boxing Day 1962, City won at Southend United and then lost at home to the same opponents three days later – before the Big Freeze wiped out the League programme until March.

1   Which City player was sent off in the 2–1 home win over Doncaster Rovers on 29 December 2004?

2   Who were the visitors for City's record Boxing Day home crowd of 40,231? And in which season?

3   With which team did City famously share eight goals on Boxing Day 1970?

4   Which player scored City's last festive hat-trick, in a 3–1 win over Doncaster Rovers on 28 December 2003?

5   Which team, who later dropped the prefix from their name, were City's first Christmas Day opponents in 1905?

6   Against which current non-League side from Lancashire did City record their only post-war Christmas Day-Boxing Day double in 1947?

7   Which striker scored on his debut as City won 3–2 at Portsmouth on 3 January 2011?

8   Which current Conference League team provided the opposition for City's last Christmas Day fixture in 1957?

9   Who were the opponents for City's furthest home and away festive fixtures?

10 Who scored two goals as City beat the then Swansea Town 4–1 in 1966, to record a first New Year's Day post-war win?

11 Who scored the winner in City's last New Year's Day victory, 2–1 over Huddersfield Town, in 2005?

And Finally ...

The beauty of the League Cup is that it is impossible to be humiliated by a non-League side. City still pioneer the notion of concentrating on the League, and have managed to exit the competition at the hands of a few sides who have spent more time outside the Football League than in it. But there have been a couple of finals in the even more obscure competitions.

1   City's first Cup Final came in the Watney Cup in 1973. Who beat them?

2   How many Scottish sides did City face during their four campaigns in the Anglo-Scottish Cup?

3   Who were City's first opponents in the League Cup?

4   Which midfielder – a record signing when he joined
     City – scored against Lazio and Verona in the Tigers' sole
     season in the Anglo-Italian Cup?

5   In which competition did City reach the inaugural final,
     losing 2–1 against Bournemouth at Boothferry Park in
     May 1984?

6   Who were City's League Cup first-round opponents in
     four out of five seasons, from 1980/81 to 1984/85?

7   Which now defunct Football League side ended City's
     League Cup hopes at the first-round stage in the 1994/95
     and 1996/97 tournaments?

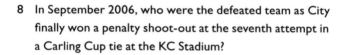

8　In September 2006, who were the defeated team as City finally won a penalty shoot-out at the seventh attempt in a Carling Cup tie at the KC Stadium?

9　In the LDV Vans Trophy, who scored a hat-trick against Leigh RMI in October 2001 – City's first in competitive matches other than League or FA Cup contests?

10　Who scored the away goal at Crystal Palace, which earned a shock League Cup victory for City in September 1997?

11　And finally, which team was relegated from the Football League in the 2011/12 season, but still proved too good for City in the first round of that season's League Cup?

THE ANSWERS

Cup Glory

1 Luton Town in December 1998.

2 A perimeter wall collapsed.

3 Hednesford Town.

4 Blyth Spartans.

5 Keith Edwards.

6 Scarborough's McCain Stadium.

7 Arsenal.

8 The General Election.

9 Grimethorpe United.

10 Chelsea in the 1999/2000 season.

11 Darlington.

Fer Ark

1 The other letters had fallen off the sign above the supermarket.

2 Jacksons Grandways.

3 Alan Hardaker.

4 Lincoln City, 0–0.

5 Golf.

6 Floodlight pylons.

7 Darlington.

8 Michael Ingham.

9 Macclesfield Town.

10 Martyn's famous 'This Is Boothferry Park' introduction.

11 Everton.

1 Liverpool, with 25,030 on 3 May 2010.

2 Ben Burgess, against Kidderminster Harriers on 26 April 2003.

3 Ian Ashbee.

4 Walsall.

5 Chelsea.

6 Burnley, with four.

7 Mark Clattenburg.

8 Raich Carter.

9 Leon Cort.

10 The Premier League bell broke when he rang it.

11 Elton John.

Our Guests

1 Show jumping.

2 Craig Brown.

3 Alf Ramsey.

4 Elland Road was closed as a sanction for crowd trouble.

5 Spain.

6 Baseball.

7 The Harlem Globetrotters.

8 The Yorkshire Cup.

9 Lashings.

10 Robin van Persie.

11 The Who.

1   The National Hockey Stadium.

2   Andy Flounders.

3   Ray Henderson.

4   Alan Smith.

5   Fellows Park, Walsall.

6   Colchester United.

7   Coventry City.

8   Dean Windass.

9   Leeds Road, Huddersfield.

10   Twerton Park, Bath, home of Bristol Rovers.

11   Saltergate, Chesterfield.

Easy Balls

1 Scarborough.

2 Billy Whitehurst.

3 Tim Wilby.

4 The Watney Cup.

5 Peter Swan.

6 Grimsby Town.

7 Ian Goodison.

8 Chester City.

9 Caleb Folan from Wigan Athletic, August 2007.

10 Matty Fryatt.

11 Nottingham Forest.

Fish

1 Martin Fish.

2 Rodney Rowe.

3 Russell Fry.

4 Steve Guppy.

5 Gary Gill.

6 Andy Flounders.

7 Bernard Fisher.

8 Mick Milner.

9 Jimmy Bullard.

10 Paul Musslewhite.

11 Peter Taylor.

Battered

1 Carlisle United.

2 Brian Little.

3 Richard Peacock and Neil Mann.

4 Five: Ken Wagstaff, Chris Chilton, Ken Houghton, Ian Butler and Ray Henderson.

5 Ryan France.

6 Theodore Whitmore.

7 Linton Brown.

8 Wayne Brown.

9 Billy Bly.

10 Bryan Hughes.

11 Mike Edwards.

Gaffers

1 Colin Appleton.

2 Mark Hateley.

3 Jan Molby.

4 John Kaye, Bobby Collins and Ken Houghton.

5 Three.

6 Frank Buckley

7 Brian Horton.

8 Cliff Britton, from July 1961 until July 1970.

9 Mike Smith.

10 Rochdale.

11 Peter Taylor.

Striking Tigers

1 Motherwell.

2 Oxford United.

3 Andy Payton.

4 Kevin Francis.

5 Ken Wagstaff.

6 Coventry City.

7 Danny Allsopp.

8 Bill Bradbury.

9 David Brown.

10 Stan Mortensen.

11 Two.

Between The Sticks

1 Peter Skipper.

2 Ian McKechnie.

3 Aston Villa.

4 Billy Bly.

5 Macclesfield Town.

6 Sergio Leite.

7 Jeff Wealands.

8 Tony Norman.

9 Andy Oakes.

10 Wigan Athletic.

11 Iain Hesford.

Long Punts

1   Denis Law.

2   Garreth Roberts.

3   Southend United.

4   Brian Little.

5   He became the first player to be sent off in an FA Cup
    semi-final.

6   An E-Type Jaguar.

7   It was the first Football League match to be played at
    Boothferry Park on a Sunday.

8   An outbreak of polio in the local community.

9   5p.

10 Three Crowns.

11 It was foggy and he didn't realise the match had been
    abandoned.

We Are Premier League

1 Geovanni.

2 Just two – Boaz Myhill and Matt Duke.

3 Andy Dawson.

4 September 2008.

5 Fulham.

6 Damien Duff.

7 Michael Turner.

8 Daniel Cousin.

9 Portsmouth.

10 George Boateng.

11 Mark Cullen.

1 Kevin Kilbane.

2 Stephen Hunt.

3 Jermain Defoe, Fernando Torres, Wayne Rooney.

4 Marlon King.

5 Geovanni.

6 Kamil Zayatte.

7 Wayne Rooney.

8 Dean Windass.

9 George Boateng, against Blackburn Rovers in February
   2010 and Arsenal the following month.

10 Thirteen.

11 Kevin Kilbane.

Yorkshire's Number One?

1 Jon Parkin.

2 Scunthorpe United.

3 Leeds United.

4 Auto Windscreens Shield.

5 Doncaster Rovers.

6 Nick Barmby.

7 Sheffield United.

8 Dean Marney.

9 Huddersfield Town.

10 Scarborough.

11 City fans were moved from the South Stand seats and terrace to accommodate more visiting supporters.

1 Stan Mortensen.

2 Jan Vennegoor of Hesselink.

3 Kevin Kilbane.

4 Richard Garcia.

5 Jay-Jay Okocha.

6 Theodore Whitmore.

7 Robert Koren (Slovenia).

8 Jan Molby.

9 Mark Hateley.

10 Billy Bremner.

11 Jozy Altidore.

Tiger Nations

1   Viggo Jensen.

2   Clint Marcelle.

3   Richard Sneekes.

4   Antonio Doncel-Varcarcel, although not many people
    bothered with the last bit.

5   Henrik Pedersen.

6   Stelios Giannakopoulos.

7   Peru.

8   Bolton Wanderers.

9   Feyenoord.

10 Gabon.

11 Peter Halmosi.

England
Expects

1 Don Revie.

2 Steve Moran.

3 Derby County.

4 Saudi Arabia.

5 Emlyn Hughes.

6 Scotland.

7 Neil Franklin.

8 Jimmy Bullard.

9 Moldova and Spain.

10 David Beckham.

11 Stuart Pearson.

Home Internationals

1 Bobby Collins.

2 United States.

3 Paul McShane.

4 MK Dons.

5 Former jockey John Francome.

6 Bolton Wanderers.

7 Glyn Hodges.

8 Tom Cairney.

9 Iain Dowie.

10 Stephen Hunt.

11 Olympiakos.

Tap-Ins

1 Tom Belton.

2 The Billy Bly Trophy.

3 FC Vasas.

4 Tommy Docherty.

5 Dr Death.

6 Tony Norman.

7 Tampa Bay Rowdies.

8 Ian Botham.

9 Dean Windass.

10 Stuart Elliott.

11 Ian Ashbee.

Club Connections

1 Plymouth Argyle.

2 Sunderland.

3 Carlisle United.

4 Sheffield Wednesday.

5 Bristol Rovers.

6 Charlton Athletic.

7 Everton.

8 Hartlepool United.

9 Crewe Alexandra.

10 Manchester City.

11 Swansea City.

Loan Stars

1   David Rocastle.

2   Martin Carruthers.

3   Brad Guzan and Vito Mannone.

4   Mark Noble.

5   Neil Clement.

6   Kyle Lightbourne.

7   Gary Ablett.

8   Seyi Olofinjana.

9   Steven Boyack.

10   Colin Alcide.

11   Ibrahima Sonko.

The Nearly Men

1   Juninho.

2   Alvaro Negredo.

3   D.J. Campbell.

4   Michael Owen.

5   Alan Ball.

6   Gary Megson.

7   Stuart Pearce.

8   Frank Stapleton.

9   Mick Jones.

10   Emile Heskey.

11   Fraizer Campbell.

Round 24 — Tiger Teeth

1 Andy 'Jock' Davidson.

2 Billy Whitehurst.

3 Gary Brabin.

4 George Boateng.

5 Brian Horton.

6 Ian Ashbee.

7 Jason van Blerk.

8 Justin Whittle.

9 Jon Whitney.

10 Curtis Woodhouse.

11 Jimmy Lodge.

Tiger Tantrums

1 Marlon King.

2 While warming up on the touchline he interfered with Rory Delap's long-throw run-up.

3 Cesc Fàbregas.

4 Tennis balls.

5 Warren Joyce.

6 Scunthorpe United.

7 The Women's Institute.

8 Slovenia.

9 The Hull City steam locomotive name plate.

10 David Lloyd.

11 City of Manchester Stadium, now Etihad Stadium.

Crunching Tackles

1 Doncaster Rovers.

2 The Faroe Islands.

3 Terry Dolan and Stan Ternent.

4 Trevor Bugg.

5 Guernsey.

6 Notts County at The Boulevard.

7 Bermuda.

8 Leicester City.

9 Motherwell.

10 Fulham.

11 Craig Fagan.

Tigers on TV

1   Middlesbrough.

2   Bradley Orr.

3   Arsenal. Away. We won 2–1. WE WON 2–1!

4   Tottenham Hotspur.

5   Sheffield Wednesday.

6   Gareth Barry.

7   Setanta.

8   Hearts.

9   Preston North End.

10   Brian Marwood.

11   Stoke City.

Celebrity Tigers

1   Sir Tom Courtenay.

2   Omar Sharif.

3   Mark Robinson.

4   Sarah Beeny.

5   Billy Whitehurst.

6   The Beautiful South.

7   John Alderton.

8   Alan Plater.

9   Roy North.

10   Stephen Malkmus.

11   Bertie Ahern.

Christmas Crackers

I   Nick Barmby.

2   Millwall in the 1965/66 season.

3   Sheffield Wednesday.

4   Jason Price.

5   Burslem Port Vale.

6   Southport.

7   Matty Fryatt.

8   Gateshead.

9   Millwall.

10   Ken Wagstaff.

II   Aaron Wilbraham.

1 Stoke City.

2 None.

3 Bolton Wanderers.

4 Ken Knighton.

5 Associate Members Cup.

6 Lincoln City.

7 Scarborough.

8 Hartlepool United.

9 Gary Alexander.

10 Ian Wright.

11 Macclesfield Town.

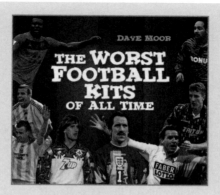

The Worst Football Kits of All Time

DAVE MOOR

978 0 7524 5904 2

In the mad, money-driven world of football, some rather interesting and sometimes shocking kits have been worn upon the field of play. This book is a full-colour celebration of some of the most outrageous strips foisted upon the poor players and the loyal fans, from clashing colours and disastrous designs to surprising sponsors and bad luck omens. With some classics and some surprises too, *The Worst Football Kits of All Time* is set to delight fans young and old, from strips donned by Victorian gentleman to modern-day prima donnas. So which really is the worst? You decide…

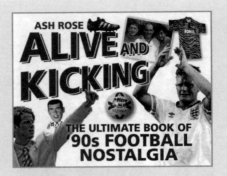

Alive and Kicking: The Ultimate Book of '90s Football Nostalgia

ASH ROSE

978 0 7524 8273 6

Whether it be stickers or Subbuteo, match programmes or 'pogs', TV shows or table football, every fan's favourite piece of football '90s nostalgia is collected in this fun look back at the beautiful game's most treasured mementoes, moments and memorabilia, from a decade that changed football. From the fun to the farcical, classic to cringe, everything football fans hold dear to their hearts is included in one place for the very first time!

Alive and Kicking is the perfect companion to any football fan who grew up singing 'Three Lions', swapping stickers in a cold playground or playing video games on a 16-bit console. If the 1990s are now retro, then this is your retro celebration of everything that was football in that memorable decade.